REPRODUCTIVE SYSTEM

LORRIE KLOSTERMAN

Marshall Cavendish
Benchmark

Marshall Cavendish Benchmark

99 White Plains Road

Tarrytown, New York 10591

www.marshallcavendish.us

All websites were available and accurate when this book was sent to press.

Editor: Karen Ang

Publisher: Michelle Bisson

Art Director: Anahid Hamparian

Series Design by: Kay Petronio

Series Designer: Elynn Cohen

Library of Congress Cataloging-in-Publication Data

Klosterman, Lorrie.

The reproductive system / By Lorrie Klosterman.

p. cm. -- (The amazing human body)

Includes bibliographical references and index.

Summary: "Discusses the parts that make up the human reproductive system, what can go wrong, how to treat those illnesses and diseases, and how to stay healthy"--Provided by publisher.

ISBN 978-0-7614-4041-3

1. Human reproduction--Juvenile literature. 2. Generative organs--Juvenile literature. I. Title.

QP251.5.K56 2010   612.6--dc22   2008037256

This book is not intended for use as a substitute for advice, consultation, or treatment by a licensed medical practitioner. The reader is advised that no action of a medical nature should be taken without consultation with a licensed medical practitioner, including action that may seem to be indicated by the contents of this work, since individual circumstances vary and medical standards, knowledge, and practices change with time. The publisher, author, and medical consultants disclaim all liability and cannot be held responsible for any problems that may arise from use of this book.

 = tubules of sperm in the epididymis

Front cover: A fetus developing inside the womb, or uterus   Back Cover: An unfertilized ovum

Photo research by Tracey Engel

Front cover photo: Yoav Levy / Alamy

The photographs in this book are used by permission and through the courtesy of: Getty: 3DClinic, 6, 39; Margo Silver, 11; OMG, 14; NucleusMedicalArt.com, 16, 20, 21, 24, 27, 30, 31, 44, 45, 47; Yorgos Nikas, 18, 42, back cover; Jana Leon, 46; Ed White, 48; Dr. David Phillips, 4, 50; DR. Fred Hossler, 52; Dorling Kindersley, 57; 3D4Medical.com, 60; Spike Walker, 62; Olver Strewe, 63; Tricia Shay/NonStock, 71. Alamy: Science Photo Library: 7; Gopal Murti, 9; Phil Degginger, 12; DocCheck Medical Services, 13; Universal Images Group Limited, 17, 34, 41; Judith Glick, 25; Science Photo Library, 29; Nucleus Medical Art, Inc., 37, 69; Kumar Sriskandan, 66; MedicalRF.com, 68. Photo Researchers: SPL, 19; James Cavallini, 23; John R. Foster, 43; Dr. P. Marazzi, 55; Veronique Burger, 58; Scott Camazine, 59; Dr. Tony Brain, 61; Hugh Turvey, 64. SuperStock: Image Source, 1, 28, 38.

Printed in Malaysia

123456

CONTENTS

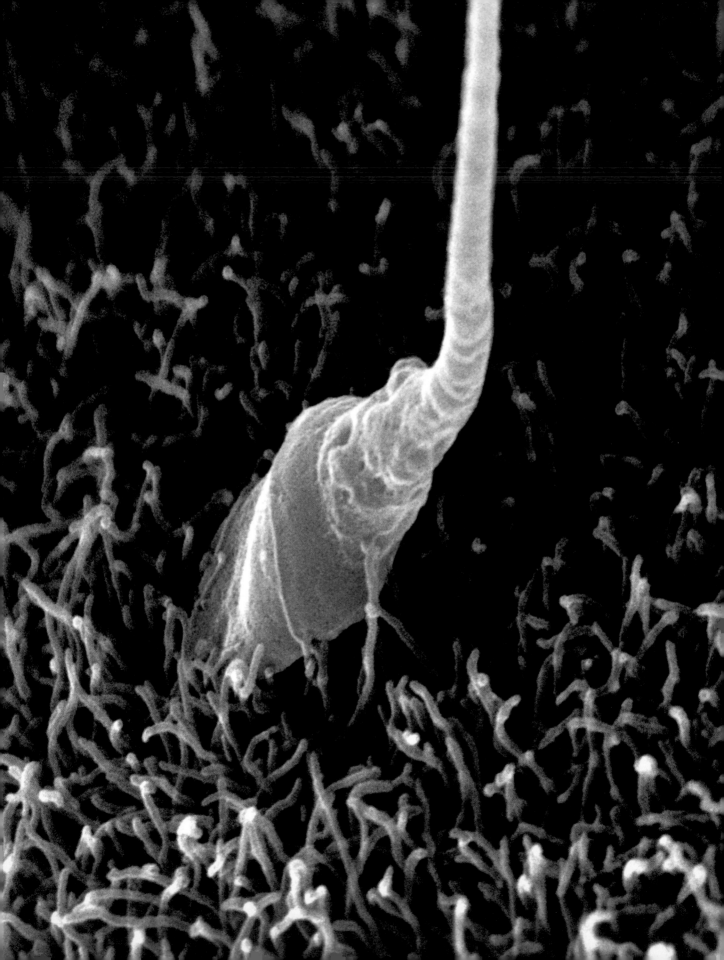

1

What Is the Reproductive System?

The reproductive system refers to those parts of the body that are necessary to create a baby. Unlike other systems of the body—such as the respiratory system, which allows us to breathe—the reproductive system is not needed for keeping someone alive. However, the reproductive system is essential to keeping the human population going. Generation after generation, new people are born because of the activities of the reproductive system.

It is important that people know the facts about how their bodies work, which includes all the different body systems. By learning about their bodies, people can do what they can to stay healthy and get

A sperm enters an egg to begin the process of fertilization and reproduction.

medical help when there is a problem. It is especially important for people to understand the reproductive system, since it is involved in pregnancy and sexually transmitted diseases.

TWO GENDERS

The bodies of females and males are alike in many ways, but their reproductive systems are quite different. Like nearly every living organism, two genders—female and male—are needed for reproduction. Two genders are made possible by genetics and reproductive hormones. Genetics refers to the genetic material, also called DNA, that is present in every cell of the body. DNA controls many things about a person, including gender. DNA is in charge of how a fetus forms in its mother's womb, and a certain portion of that DNA controls whether the fetus forms a male or female reproductive system.

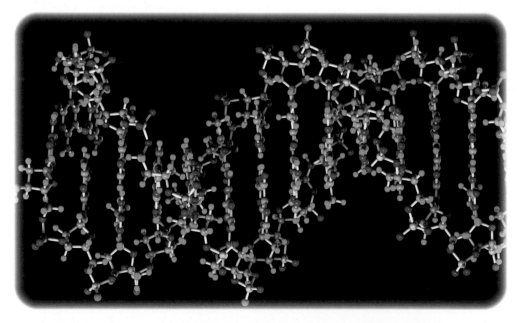

This computer image of DNA shows the molecule's structure, which is called a double helix.

CHROMOSOMES AND GENDER

When a baby is born, he or she already has the reproductive organs of a male or female. Special portions of DNA, called sex chromosomes, are in charge of how a developing fetus's reproductive organs form. Each person has a pair of sex chromosomes. In a girl, the two sex chromosomes are very similar to each other. Each is called an "X" chromosome. They guide the formation of a female reproductive system. A boy's sex chromosomes are different. One of the pair is an X and the other is a much smaller Y chromosome. The Y chromosome causes the fetus to form a male reproductive system.

Every so often a fetus will have an extra sex chromosome, or will be missing one. The most common abnormality is having a Y and two or more Xs. Someone with that set of sex chromosomes looks male, but is infertile, which means he cannot make babies. On the other hand, someone with an X and two Ys looks male and is usually fertile.

Sometimes a fetus with a normal sex chromosome number develops abnormally because the mother was exposed to sex steroids during pregnancy. For instance, if she is carrying a fetus with two X chromosomes, but takes medications that contain male-type sex steroids, the fetus may develop male reproductive organs.

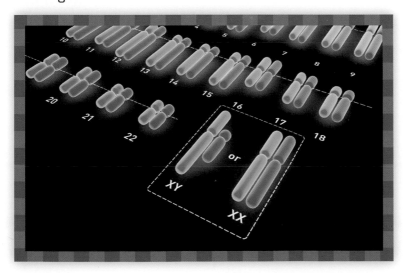

Reproductive hormones also have an important role to play in gender. They are chemicals that travel through the bloodstream and influence what is happening in the reproductive organs. Reproductive hormones become plentiful during the stage in childhood called puberty, which usually happens in the early to middle teenage years. During puberty, a child's body visibly changes into that of a young woman or a young man, and reproductive organs mature. Reproductive hormones nurture these changes. A group of hormones called sex steroids are especially important in gender. Males make more of one kind of sex steroid (testosterone), and females make more of another (estrogen). So while the basic body plan of male or female is set by genetics, hormones ensure that each gender matures fully.

TWO GAMETES

Each gender's reproductive organs make very special cells called gametes. Gametes hold genetic information needed to create a baby. A female's gametes are called eggs, or ova (singular, ovum). A male's gametes are called spermatozoa, or sperm. Eggs and sperm are quite different from each other, and they must come together in order to start a new life. Almost every part of the reproductive system helps in some way to make eggs or sperm, or to ensure that an egg and sperm can meet.

A very young person does not yet make mature eggs or sperm. Instead, there are immature versions of them in an infant's and a young child's body. Only during puberty are fully mature eggs and sperm made for the first time. That happens because hormones that control reproduction become abundant during puberty. The hormones spur the immature cells to change into eggs or sperm.

Descendants

As a person ages, and then finally dies, the body's cells die, too. But gametes—eggs or sperm—are unlike any other cell in the body. They are

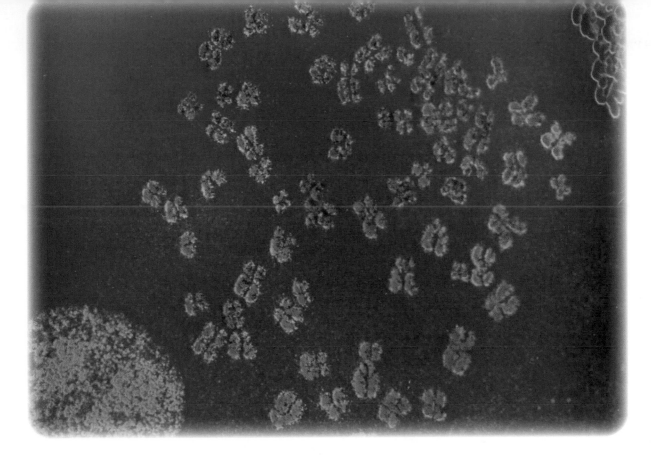

The X-shaped objects in this magnified image are human chromosomes.

a living link that sparks the next generation and keeps the human race going in an unbroken chain. An egg, for instance, is made in a woman's ovaries. If an egg is fertilized by a man's sperm, it can develop into a new human being. When that new person reaches adulthood, he or she makes eggs or sperm, too. Those gametes can create a child as well, and so on. In this way, generations replace each other.

At the same time, parents are passing along their genetic material (DNA) to the next generation. Eggs and sperm each contain a sampling of the parent's genetic material—exactly half the amount needed to make a complete person. So when egg and sperm combine at fertilization, each brings half of the genetic material that will guide the development of the child. In this way, gametes are what makes children look similar, but not identical to, their parents. Only gametes, of all living cells, directly connect children to parents, and to grandparents, and great-grandparents, and all the ancestors who came before them.

PUBERTY: FROM CHILD TO ADULT

A young person's body changes in many ways during the teenage years. That period of time, called puberty, is when the reproductive system becomes fully active for the first time. Puberty starts around the ages of twelve to fourteen, and lasts a few years. However, some people go through puberty at a young age, even before reaching the teen years.

Puberty is controlled by reproductive hormones made by the brain and the gonads (testes and ovaries). The hormones become more abundant during puberty than ever before. They are carried throughout the body in the bloodstream, and cause many parts of a young person's body to change.

During puberty, boys develop into young men, usually with the first signs of a beard and moustache. Their faces look more angular as bones in the jaw and under the eyebrows grow. Their voices deepen because their larynxes, or voice boxes, grow larger, and their muscles become larger and stronger. Girls go through changes that make them look like mature women. Their breasts develop, and their hips and thighs become more rounded as they begin to store a bit more fat beneath the skin. A girl's pelvis, which are the bones in the hip area, grows wider. This will make it easier for her to give birth to a baby if she becomes pregnant.

Other changes at puberty happen to both boys and girls. Hair under their arms becomes coarse and visible, and new kinds of sweat glands become active there. Hair on the arms and legs becomes more noticeable, too. Coarse hair appears around the genitals, which grow to adult size during puberty. In addition, boys and girls reach their adult height as their bones go through a final growth phase. These outward changes are a clear sign that the reproductive system is maturing inside as well.

During puberty, young men develop hair on places, such as the face, chest, armpits, and groin.

THE POWER OF HORMONES

A woman's ovaries and a man's testes are most known for the very special cells they make: eggs and sperm. But hormones known as sex steroids are also made by those organs. Follicles in the ovary make estrogen and progesterone, the most abundant sex steroids in women. The hormones stimulate her uterus, vagina, genitalia, and breasts to grow and mature.

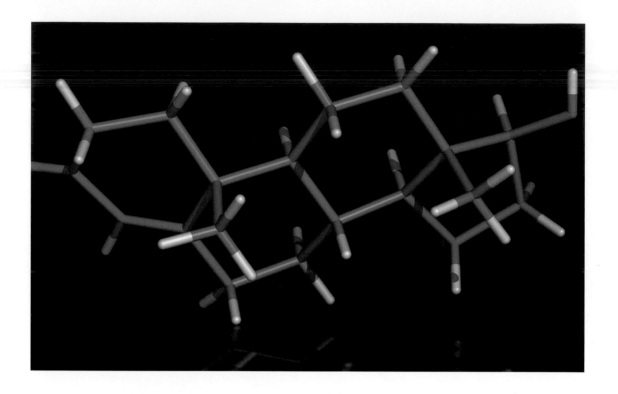

This computer-generated image shows the chemical structure of testosterone.

Testes make male sex steroids, mostly testosterone, which acts on a boy's body to make muscle and bone grow, and hair to grow on the face and body.

Usually, each person makes the type of sex steroids that match the reproductive organs he or she was born with. But sometimes not enough sex steroids are made, and gender features do not fully mature. A female with little estrogen will not develop breasts and will probably not be able to have children, because her internal reproductive organs will not mature. A male who makes little or no testosterone will not have much male-type growth of his muscles, bones, and body hair, and his voice will remain more like that of a child's because the larynx will not grow much.

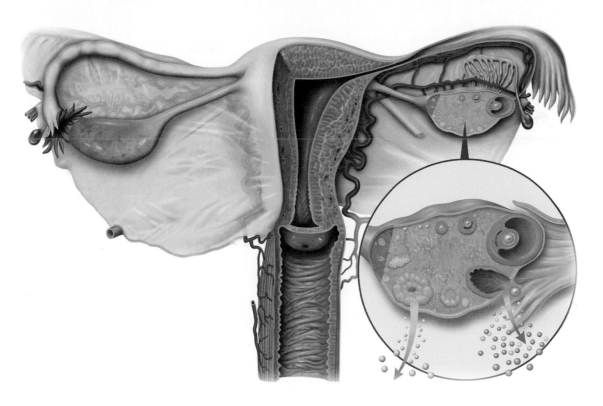

One job of the ovaries is to produce sex hormones, such as estrogen (blue) and progesterone (yellow).

In fact, in centuries past, some boys who had beautiful singing voices were intentionally castrated—had their testes removed—to prevent their voices from changing at puberty. Most people who lack sex steroids are easily treated with medications that replace the needed hormones.

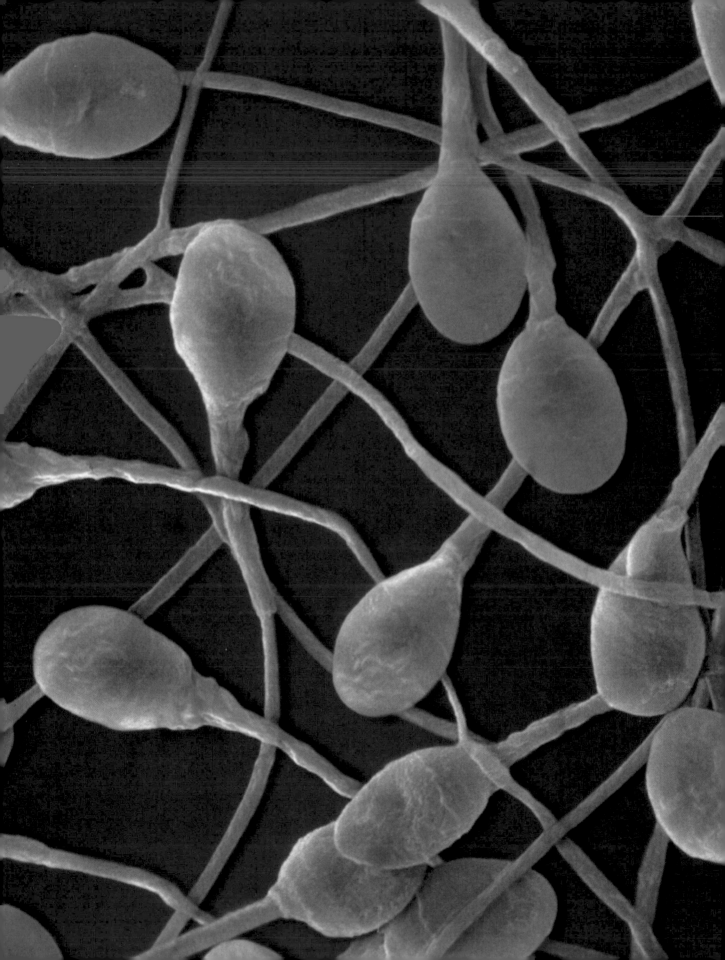

2

The Parts of the Reproductive System

A special team of cells, organs, and chemicals carries out the tasks of the reproductive system. Some of the reproductive system's parts are visible on the outside, but most are inside.

THE FEMALE REPRODUCTIVE SYSTEM

The female system consists of the ovaries, where eggs are made, a pair of tubes and other organs through which eggs travel or are held during

The reproductive system is made up of many different parts, from ovaries and testes to eggs and sperm (shown here).

pregnancy, and genitalia and breasts, which are visible on the outside of the body.

Ovaries

Eggs are made in a pair of organs called ovaries. Each ovary is about the size of an almond, and is nestled in the lowest part of the abdomen, one on the left side and one on the right side. The ovaries are within the pelvis. The pelvis is like a protective cage made of strong bones. Some parts of the pelvis, such as the hipbones, are easy to feel or see beneath the skin on either side of the body, just below the navel, or belly button.

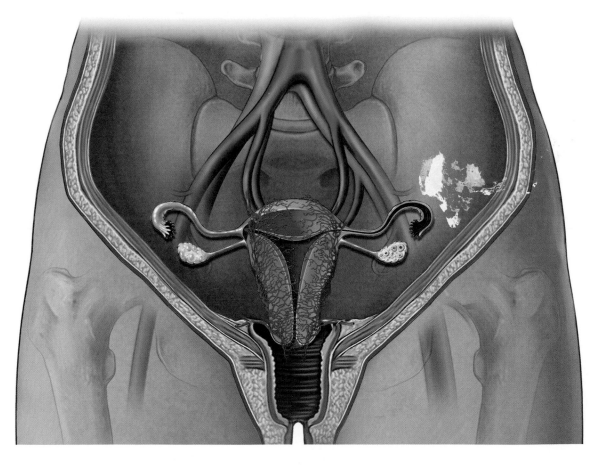

Many blood vessels provide blood and other nutrients to female reproductive organs, such as the uterus and ovaries.

Inside each ovary are thousands of immature eggs. The eggs are larger than most cells, but even so, they are too small to be seen without the aid of a microscope. Each egg is grouped with other kinds of cells from the ovary, which completely surround the egg like hands cupping a tiny ball. Together, an egg and the cells around it are called a follicle. Follicle cells shuttle nutrients, water, and other necessary materials to the egg. In addition, follicle cells make the female sex steroids, estrogen and progesterone in different quantities at different times.

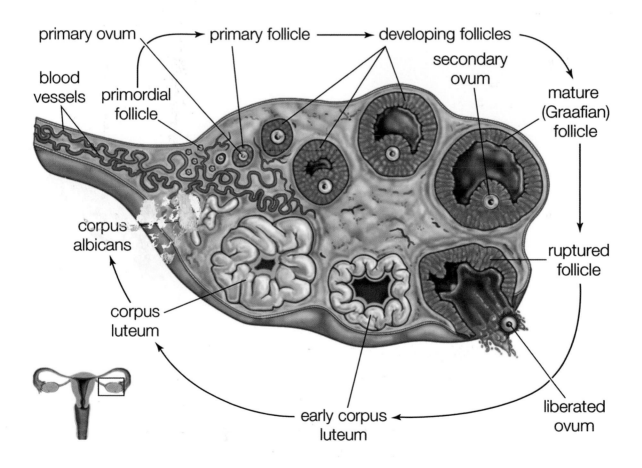

This illustration shows the different steps of ovulation, as a follicle and an ovum develop and mature. .

In the ovary of a mature woman, or a teenage girl nearing the end of puberty, some follicles are in the process of growing and maturing. In a growing follicle, the cells around the egg become more plentiful and collect in many layers. Fluid collects in the follicle, making it grow even larger. The egg grows only a little in size, and remains invisible to the naked eye even when fully mature. Ovaries with growing follicles look bumpy on the surface because the largest follicles bulge out. Once a month, one of the largest follicles develops a tear on its outer surface. It breaks open, and fluid rushes out, carrying the egg with it. The release of an egg from its follicle is known as ovulation.

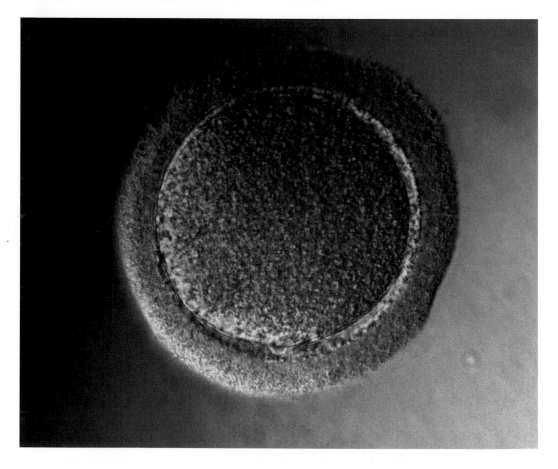

This mature ovum, or egg, cannot be seen with the naked eye—a microscope is needed to view it.

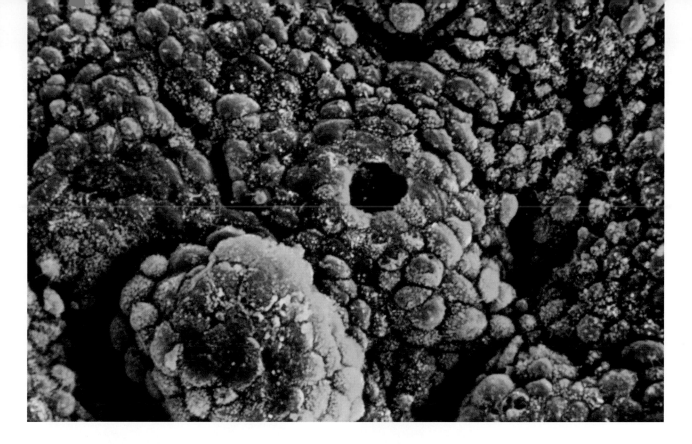

The body may use the cells of the corpus luteum to nourish a fertilized egg that is developing into a fetus.

After the egg is released, the follicle from which it came collapses into a mass of cells. The mass is called a corpus luteum. Usually, cells in a corpus luteum begin to die within a few days. But if the egg that left the follicle becomes fertilized by sperm and settles in the woman's uterus, chemical signals from the uterus reach the ovary, and keep the corpus luteum cells alive for many weeks. During that time, the cells make hormones that are essential for a healthy pregnancy.

Oviducts

An egg that has escaped its ovary must travel several inches to the uterus, or womb. The egg makes that journey by passing down a tube called an oviduct, or fallopian tube. Each ovary has its own oviduct, which connects to the uterus. The end closest to the ovary is much wider and shaped like a funnel. That makes it easier for eggs to find their way into it. The oviduct

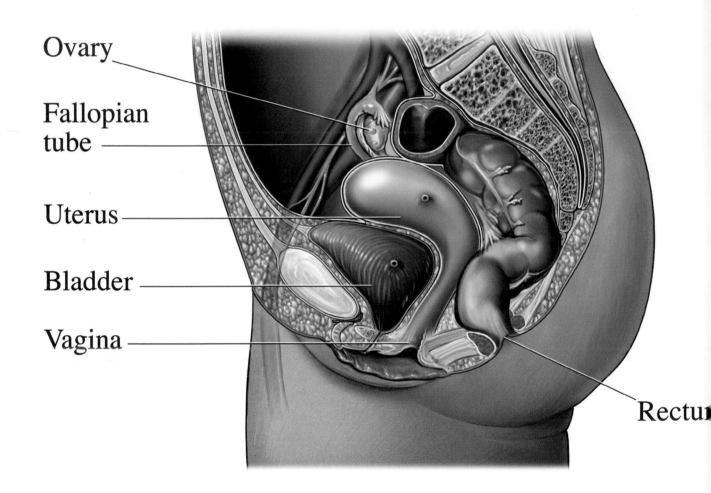

Ovary

Fallopian
tube

Uterus

Bladder

Vagina

Rectum

This illustration shows a side view of the female reproductive organs.

has bands of muscle along its length that squeeze the oviduct rhythmically, helping to move the egg along. There are also cells in the oviduct with tiny, hair like structures that move back and forth, like grass in the wind. They create a gentle flow of fluid that carries the egg along.

Uterus

The uterus, or womb, is shaped something like an upside-down pear that is hollow. The walls of the uterus, which surround the hollow area, are several layers thick. Some of the layers are muscle, which can contract strongly if a baby that has been growing inside the uterus is ready to be born. Another layer of the uterus is called the endometrium, (*endo-* means within, *-metrium* refers to uterus). This is what an egg will brush against as it passes through the uterus.

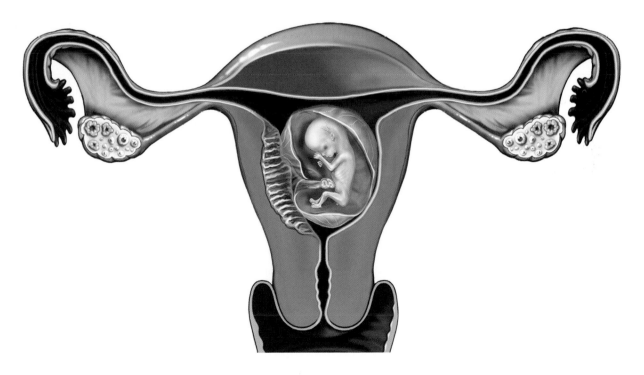

A healthy fetus develops inside a woman's uterus, or womb.

THE BRAIN IS A REPRODUCTIVE ORGAN

The brain is not usually listed as a part of the reproductive system. But it is just as important to reproduction as the other parts of the system are. For one thing, a pea-sized gland in the brain, the pituitary, makes the hormones FSH and LH, which control what the ovaries and testes are doing. The pituitary also makes the hormone prolactin, which causes a female's breasts to make milk, and oxytocin, a hormone that makes tiny muscles within the milk glands squeeze the milk out when an infant is nursing. Oxytocin also makes the uterus's muscles tighten powerfully during the birth of a baby.

The pituitary, in turn, is under the control of a neighboring brain region, called the hypothalamus. That region receives all kinds of information about what is going on in the body. In reproduction, the hypothalamus and pituitary work together to make sure the activities of the ovaries, testes, and other reproductive parts are working in harmony. The brain also has special areas where thoughts and desires about sex take place. Although many mysteries about the brain and sex remain, it seems certain that reproductive hormones influence the brain. For instance, sexual desire becomes powerful at puberty, at a time when sex steroids become plentiful. Sex steroids are known to attach to, and influence, brain cells.

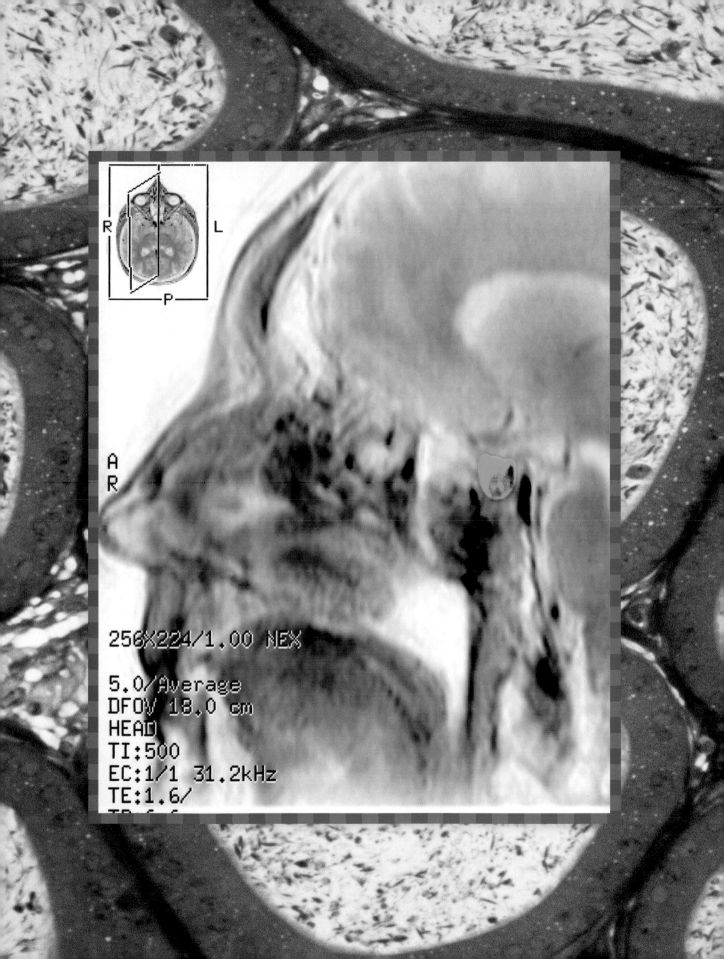

In a mature woman, the endometrium changes greatly from week to week. Sometimes it is in a brief resting state, and is just a few cells thick. It then begins to change. Within a few weeks it becomes packed with new cells, and blood vessels grow among them to keep the cells nourished with blood. Some of the cells form glands that secrete moisture and nutrients into the space within the uterus. All this makes the uterus an excellent environment for a fertilized egg that ends up in the uterus.

If no fertilized egg passes into the uterus within a week or so, the thick layers of cells are shed from the uterus. The endometrium goes through this series of changes, from a thin, resting stage to a thick layer, and back to a thin layer, every month. The process is called the menstrual cycle (named for the Latin word meaning "month"). The menstrual cycle is caused by monthly changes in the amount of reproductive hormones in a woman's bloodstream.

Vagina

The vagina is a short, wide, stretchy tube that connects the uterus to the outside of the body. The vagina has two purposes. First, it allows eggs and materials from the uterus—and a baby when it is born—to get out of the body. Second, it is where a male's penis enters during sexual intercourse, so that an egg can be fertilized inside the woman's body. There are glands in the walls of the vagina that make small amounts of a slippery liquid, which cleanses and protects the vagina from infection, and also aids in sexual intercourse.

Female Genitalia

Reproductive organs that are visible in the pubic area (between the legs) are called genitalia, or genitals. Female genitalia surround the opening of the vagina. They include a pair of skin folds nearest the vagina called the

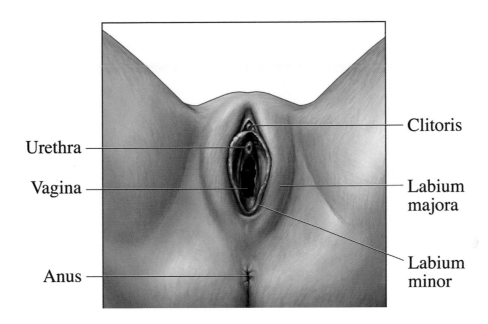

Female genitalia, such as the labia, help to protect the vagina and other female reproductive organs.

labia minora. They cover the opening to the vagina, and also to the nearby urethra (which is not a part of the reproductive system, but carries urine). The labia minora help to keep germs out. Another larger pair of skin folds is the labia majora, which enclose the labia minora. Nestled within the labia is a pea-sized genital structure called the clitoris. The clitoris is a sensitive part of the female body that gives pleasurable feelings during sexual activity.

Breasts

A woman's breasts are also part of the reproductive system. During puberty, they change and grow in response to sex steroids. Some of the growth is because fat collects in breasts, but milk-producing glands are forming, too. The glands are made of cells clustered around tiny, hollow

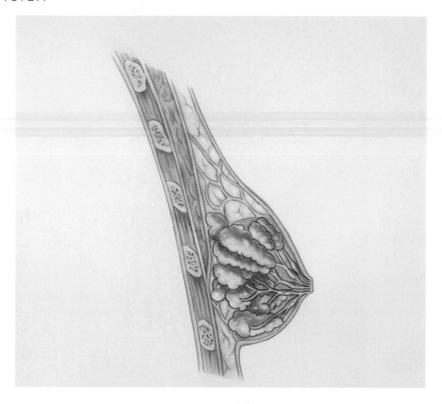

As a young woman goes through puberty, her breasts develop more fat and milk ducts.

tubes called milk ducts. When a woman becomes pregnant, her milk glands mature because of hormones her body is making. Near the end of pregnancy, her breasts are ready to start making milk. The ducts carry milk from the glands to the nipple, where the ducts open to the surface. If a woman decides to nurse her baby, the newborn would drink the milk from her breasts.

THE MALE REPRODUCTIVE SYSTEM

Testes

The male's gametes, sperm, are made in a pair of testes (singular, testis). The testes are held in a pouch of skin, called the scrotum, which is between

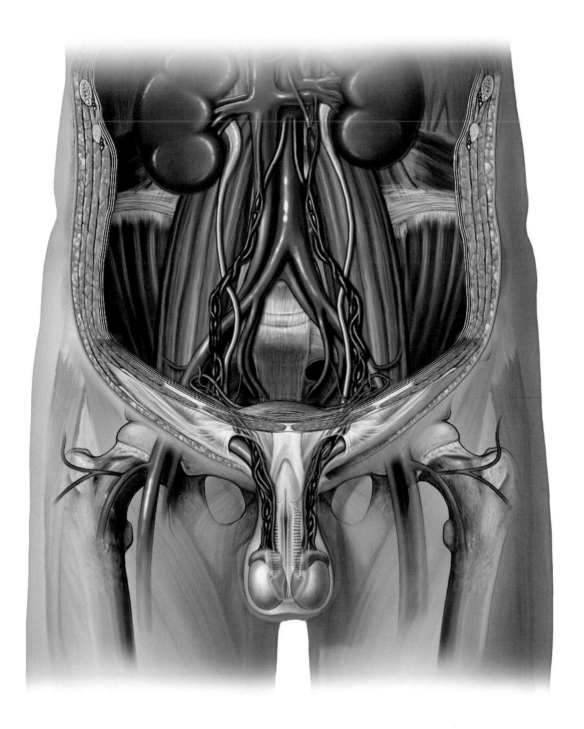

Blood vessels help nourish the testes and keep them at the right temperature, which keep the sperm alive and healthy.

and slightly in front of the legs. The testes are located there because they cannot be deep inside the body. The sperm inside the testes must be a few degrees cooler than normal body temperature. The testes of a fetus start out inside the body, in a position similar to where ovaries are in a female. In the last few months before birth, the testes gradually move, or descend, into the scrotum.

The interior of each testis is a collection of thousands of tiny tubes called seminiferous tubules (tubule means "little tube"). The tubules are coiled and packed tightly together, but there is space within them where sperm are made. Sperm are made after puberty. Before puberty, seminiferous tubules contain immature cells called spermatogonia. As the amount of reproductive hormones is a boy's bloodstream rises, the spermatogonia start making copies of themselves. Those copies of cells then develop into sperm. For the rest of a man's life, this process will continue. An average, healthy man may make billions of sperm in his lifetime.

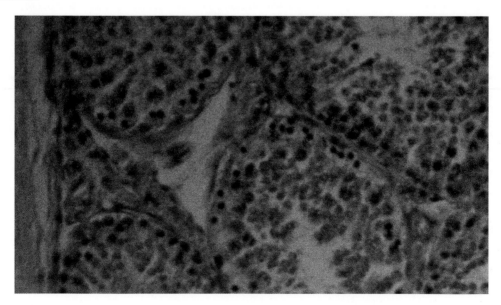

Sperm are made in the seminiferous tubules in the testis.

A magnified image shows the Sertoli cells (pink and red) that deliver nutrients to developing sperm (white).

There are other kinds of cells in the testis besides spermatogonia and developing sperm. Nestled among the sperm are very large cells, called Sertoli cells, which act like caretakers for the sperm. Sertoli cells deliver nutrients, energy molecules, water, hormones, and other important materials to the sperm as they mature. Sperm cannot live without being closely connected to a Sertoli cell. Sperm are tiny, streamlined cells with one purpose: to carry genetic material powerfully and quickly. Anything that is not needed to do that is left behind in the seminiferous tubules when the sperm move out into the male duct system. So sperm need the nutrients and other materials that the Sertoli cells provide.

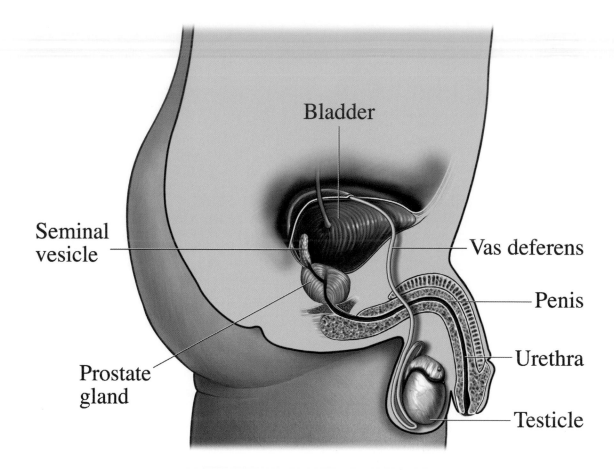

Other kinds of cells in the testis make sex steroids—specifically, the important male hormone, testosterone. These cells are located between the seminiferous tubules, not inside them.

Ductus Deferens

As sperm mature in the seminiferous tubules, they work their way out of the testis and collect in a teardrop-shaped structure called the epididymis. Each epididymis is made of tubules that connect up with the seminiferous tubules. Sperm go through a few more small changes in the epididymis, and reach full maturity.

Sperm will next travel along a hollow duct (tube), the ductus deferens (or vas deferens). Each testis has its own ductus deferens. The ductus deferentia (plural of deferens) are located inside the body, in the pelvis region. Each one connects to the urethra, which is a tube that drains urine from the bladder. The urethra carries, at different times, either urine or sperm. The urethra ends at the end of the penis. Sperm only travel through the ductus deferentia when a man reaches the most powerful point of sexual arousal, called orgasm. Then, tiny muscles that ring the ducts all along their length squeeze rhythmically, moving sperm rapidly along.

Accessory Glands

Sperm are swept along the ductus deferentia in a liquid called seminal fluid, or semen. The glands that make semen are the seminal vesicles and the prostate. These glands are located in the pelvis. Each seminal vesicle empties its contribution to semen into the nearest ductus deferens. The prostate empties its fluid into the urethra where the ductus deferentia enter it.

Semen does more than help wash sperm along. It contains a sugar called fructose, which acts as a fuel that sperm use to keep moving. Semen also has substances that cause changes in the female reproductive tract. An example is prostaglandin, which is named for the prostate gland that makes it. Prostaglandin causes muscles of the uterus and oviducts to tighten and relax rapidly, in a way that squeezes sperm up into the female system from the vagina.

One more pair of male accessory glands is the bulbourethral glands. They are located in the penis, near its tip. They make just a few drops of a clear, slippery liquid, which helps the penis slide into the female's vagina during sexual intercourse. The liquid can have living sperm in it, and can get a woman pregnant, even if the man never releases semen.

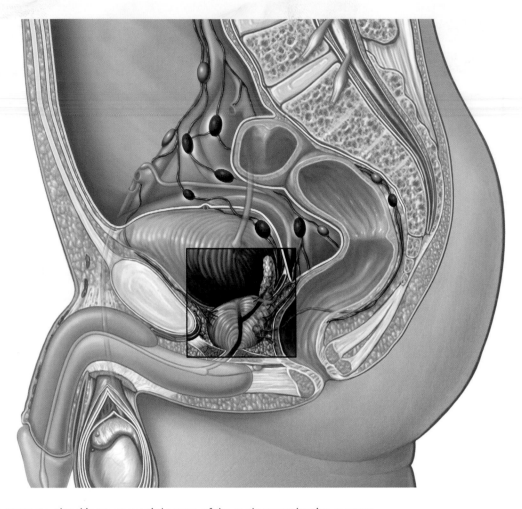

The prostate gland is an essential organ of the male reproductive system.

Male Genitalia

The male genitalia are the penis and the scrotum, a pouch of skin that holds the testes. They grow to their adult size during puberty, though they can change in size and appearance quite quickly. In cold weather or cold water, the scrotum tightens, pulling the testes close against the body for warmth. In hot weather or hot water, the scrotum relaxes. The penis, too, changes size with temperature and time of day, and when a man becomes sexually aroused. It becomes longer, wider, and firmer because blood collects in it. Those changes make it easier for the penis to enter the female's vagina and release sperm. The penis returns to its relaxed size rapidly after orgasm, or more slowly without orgasm.

WORKING TOGETHER

Each gender has certain activities in common, such as making gametes and hormones. But their bodies are designed quite differently to carry out very different roles in reproduction. A male makes sperm and delivers them into female's body, where they might contact an egg and fertilize it. A female makes eggs, provides a life-sustaining environment for a fertilized egg as it develops into a baby, and feeds the baby with breast milk after it is born. Together, the two types of reproductive systems work amazingly well to keep the human race going.

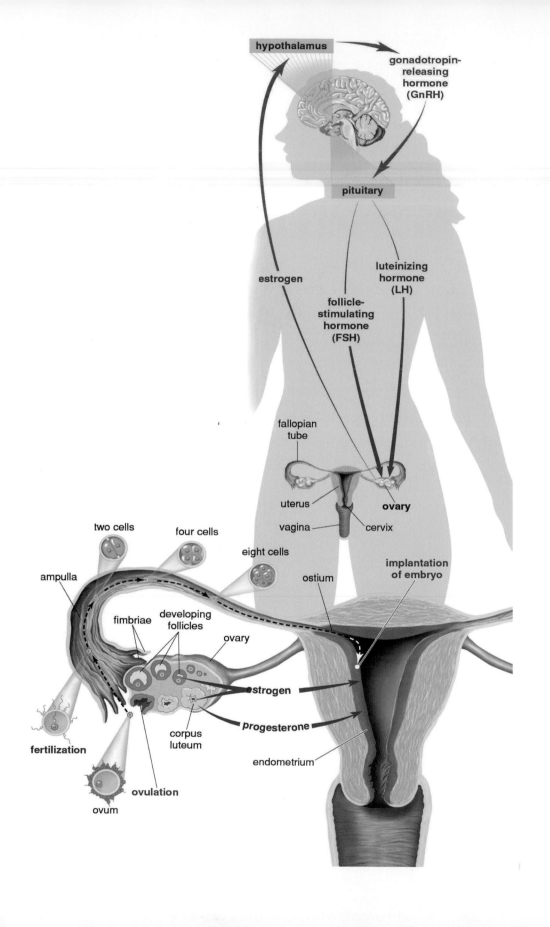

3

How the Reproductive System Works

The reproductive system is unlike other systems of the body because it needs two people to fulfill its main task: making a baby. To truly understand reproduction, one must know how the systems of each gender work, but also understand how they work together.

MAKING EGGS

From the moment a girl is born, her ovaries contain thousands of immature eggs enclosed in tiny follicles. At puberty, reproductive hormones are made in greater amounts than ever before. Two hormones

◀ *An illustration shows the hormones and processes involved in egg maturation and early pregnancy.*

made by the pituitary gland, which is in the brain, strongly influence what is happening in the ovaries. The hormones travel from the brain in the bloodstream, and get to the ovaries. One of them, follicle-stimulating hormone (FSH), does what its name says: it stimulates follicles to grow. The other, luteinizing hormone (LH), triggers ovulation of one of the largest follicles. The hormone causes to follicle to break open at the ovary's surface, releasing its egg. Sometimes more than one egg ovulates, so that two babies develop and are born at the same time, but look different from each other. These are called fraternal twins.

A woman's ovaries continue to make mature eggs for dozens of years after puberty. When she reaches her forties or fifties, though, the pituitary stops making as much FSH and LH. There are still many immature follicles in her ovaries, but without those hormones, the eggs no longer mature. A woman is said to be in menopause at that time.

The Menstrual Cycle

A woman's reproductive system works in cycles. It repeats certain activities every month. In the ovary, a new group of follicles grows each month, and one of them releases an egg. Each month, the inner lining of the uterus, the endometrium, thickens with new cells and a rich blood supply. The events in the ovary and the uterus are timed so that the egg arrives in the uterus just when the endometrium is thickest. If the egg is not fertilized, it passes through the uterus into the vagina and out of the body. Shortly afterward, the endometrium sheds the extra cells it had made that month. For about five days, cells and blood leave the uterus in a slow stream called the menstrual flow. Soon after the flow stops, the endometrium begins to build a new lush layer for the next egg.

These repeating events of the female reproductive system are called the menstrual cycle. The hormones FSH and LH, from the pituitary gland, control them. The amounts of FSH and LH rise and fall each month, setting

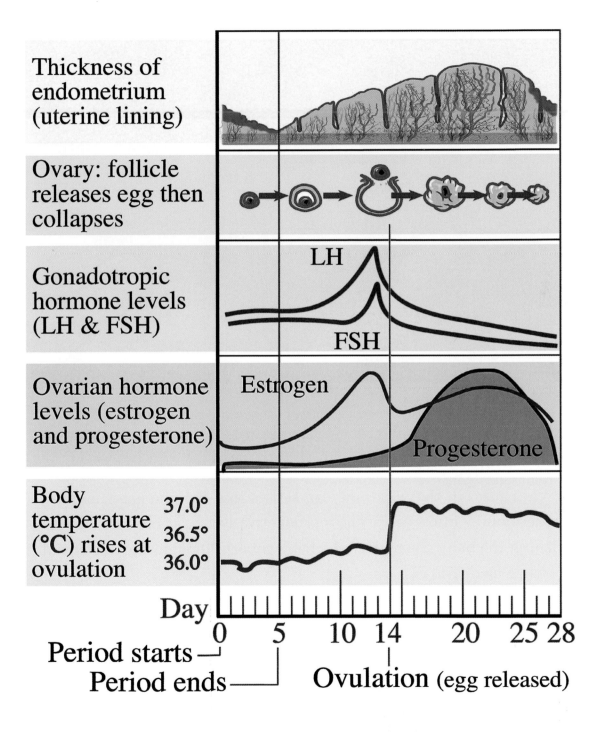

Thickness of endometrium (uterine lining)

Ovary: follicle releases egg then collapses

Gonadotropic hormone levels (LH & FSH)

LH

FSH

Ovarian hormone levels (estrogen and progesterone)

Estrogen

Progesterone

Body temperature (°C) rises at ovulation

37.0°
36.5°
36.0°

Day

0   5   10   14   20   25 28

Period starts
Period ends
Ovulation (egg released)

During the menstrual cycle, levels of sex hormones rise and fall, causing different changes in the body.

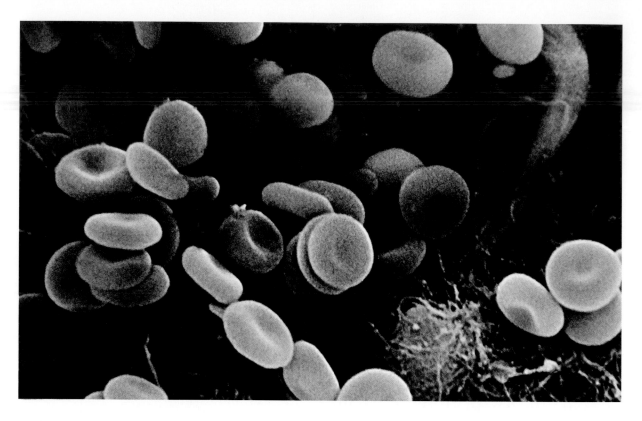

When a woman has her period, blood and cells from the endometrium are shed and exit the body through the vagina.

the timing of the cycle. Only when a fertilized egg reaches the uterus does the cycle pause. In that case, the egg settles into the endometrium and starts developing into a baby. The reproductive system's activities shift to nourishing the baby. Soon after the baby is born, though, the menstrual cycle starts up again.

MAKING SPERM

Before puberty, a boy's testes do not make sperm. But in the early teen years, FSH and LH—the hormones that get egg maturation underway in females—do the same for sperm in males. The hormones travel from the pituitary (in the brain) through the bloodstream, and when they reach the testes, spermatogonia respond by making new cells that begin the process of becoming a sperm. The cells change greatly over a few months' time, from being a round, normal-looking cell to a tiny, streamlined sperm. Each sperm has genetic material (DNA) packed tightly into a "head" region, and a hair like "tail" that can whip around and move the sperm powerfully. Most of the rest of the cell is left behind in the seminiferous tubule. Finished sperm move out of the testis and into the nearby epididymis,

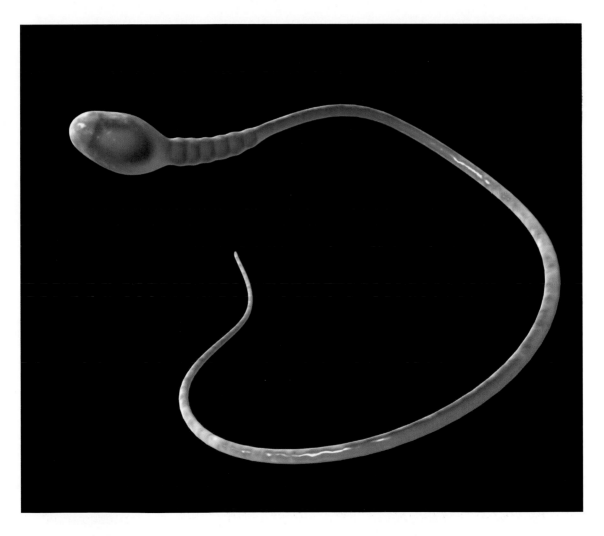

Genetic material is housed in the round head of the sperm. The sperm's long tail is used to propel it toward an egg.

where they will finish a few more steps in maturation. This process goes on continually, with new batches of cells maturing into sperm every few days.

A SPERM'S JOURNEY

Sperm must get outside a man's body to fertilize an egg. To do so, they travel from the epididymis through the ductus deferentia, into the urethra, and out the penis. The male reproductive system is well designed to get sperm moving along this journey when the man is sexually aroused, or sexually excited. That can begin when he feels sensations on his skin, especially around his genitals. Or, he may be aroused simply by thinking or even dreaming about sexual contact, or by viewing someone or something that sparks his sexual interest.

As arousal continues and builds, a man may experience orgasm. Orgasm is a surge of pleasurable feelings that also causes a sudden burst of action in the reproductive system. The epididymis and ductus deferens squeeze rhythmically and rapidly, pushing sperm toward the penis. At the same time, the semen-making organs (seminal vesicles and prostate) squeeze their fluids into the urethra, flushing sperm along it. The penis has powerful muscular contractions that push the sperm and semen from its base to its tip. The result is ejaculation--the sudden, powerful spray of semen, filled with sperm, from the penis.

SEXUAL INTERCOURSE

If a man ejaculates while his penis is inside a woman's vagina, the activity is called sexual intercourse, or simply "having sex," or "intercourse." Sperm that are released in the vagina work their way through the uterus and up into the oviducts. If a man and woman have intercourse at a time

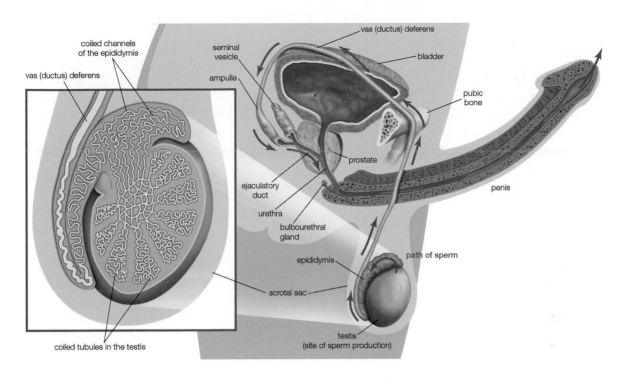

This illustration shows the structures involved in the production and movement of semen.

when an egg is traveling down the oviduct, chances are very good that she will become pregnant.

The path to an egg seems like a long and difficult one for sperm, which are the smallest of human cells. But it obviously works, since there are nearly seven billion people living on the planet today who were created that way. A sperm's tail whips rapidly, powering it along and using a sugar in semen (fructose) for energy. In addition, a woman may have an orgasm during intercourse. Just as in males, a female's orgasm makes her reproductive organs contract powerfully and rhythmically. That helps to push sperm into the uterus and oviducts.

FERTILIZATION AND IMPLANTATION

A sperm that reaches an egg must first wriggle its way through a thick coating covering the egg. The sperm's thrashing tail helps, as do special

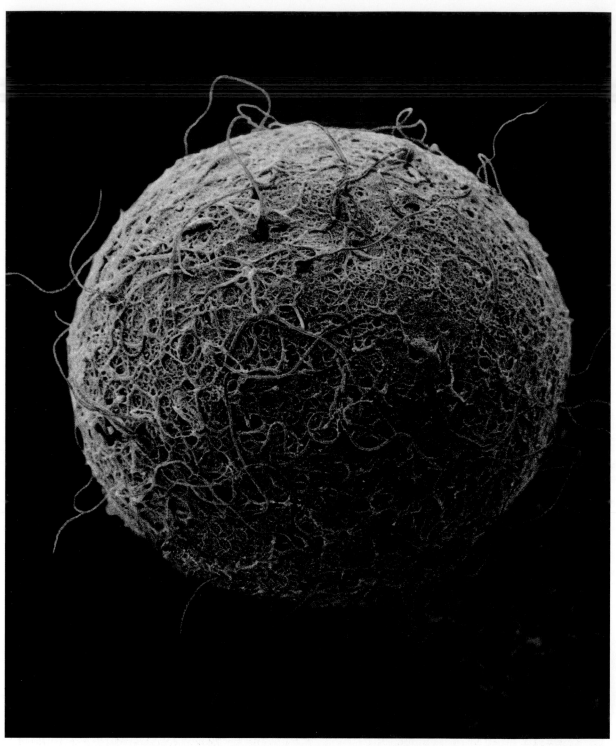

An egg (yellow) may be surrounded by many sperm (blue), but only one will enter and fertilize the egg.

A fertilized egg changes into a blastocyst as it moves down toward and attaches to the uterus.

chemicals stored in the tip of the sperm that digest a path through the coating. When the sperm's head finally contacts the egg itself, the two cells fuse, which is called fertilization. Most of the sperm's parts stay on the outside of the egg, but its precious cargo—the male's genetic material—enters the egg. Together, the egg's and the sperm's genetic material will guide the development of a new person.

A fertilized egg is called a zygote (zyg- means "yoked together," or connected to each other). During the next few days, the zygote will divide again and again, until it is a ball of many cells called a blastocyst. The blastocyst settles among the rich blood vessels and tissue of the uterus. When this happens, the blastocyst is said to be implanted. That marks the beginning of pregnancy.

THE PLACENTA

A unique living organ called the placenta forms during pregnancy. It connects a developing baby to its mother's uterus, and shuttles everything the baby needs from its mother's blood supply into its own. The placenta begins to form just a few days after a blastocyst implants in the uterus. The placenta is made by blastocyst cells and endometrial cells.

Over the nine months of pregnancy, the placenta grows into a disc-shaped organ about the size of an adult's open hand. Besides bringing life-sustaining materials to the baby, the placenta makes many substances of its own that nurture the woman's reproductive system during pregnancy. For instance, it makes a hormone very similar to the pituitary hormone LH. The placenta's version is called hCG—human chorionic gonadotropin. It gets into the mother's bloodstream and makes her ovaries make a lot of progesterone, just as LH does. That, in turn, nourishes the uterus and keeps the fetus healthy. Because hCG is made only by a placenta, it serves as a pregnancy test. It can be measured in urine

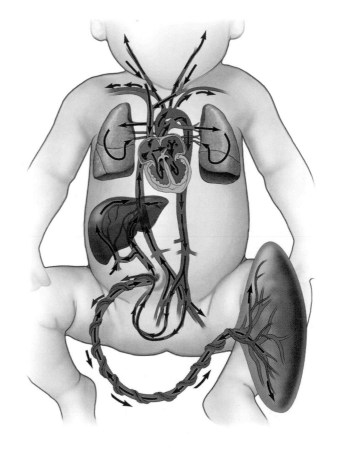

The placenta (right) brings blood and chemicals to a developing fetus.

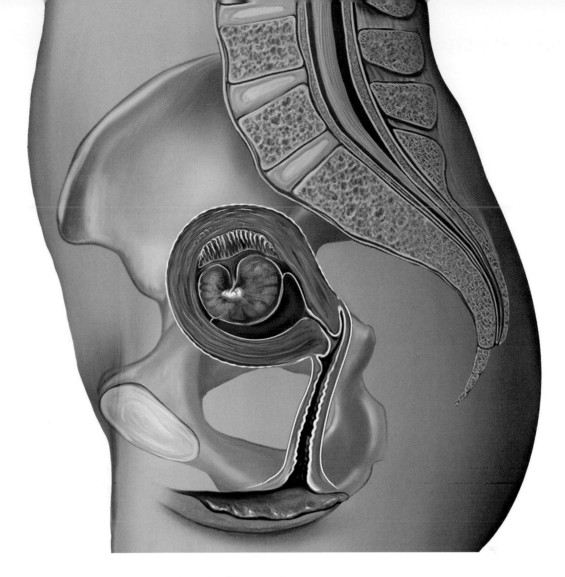

At four weeks, an embryo is only about 4 millimeters long.

or blood of a pregnant woman. This is why early pregnancy tests use blood or urine. Soon after the baby is born, the placenta is pushed out of the uterus, too. It is connected to the baby by the umbilical cord, which is cut. A person's belly button, or navel, marks the spot where the umbilical cord once was.

FROM BLASTOCYST TO BABY

It takes just about nine months for a blastocyst to become a baby that is ready to be born. During that time, the woman's whole body, not just her reproductive system, is working to provide nutrients, hormones, energy molecules, and much more for both herself and her baby. Finally, by some signal that is still not quite understood, the muscles of the uterus start to rhythmically contract every few minutes, and the process of "labor"—birthing the baby—begins.

The muscles contract more powerfully as the pituitary releases a hormone, oxytocin, in higher and higher amounts during labor. Another hormone, relaxin, helps the pelvis bones move slightly apart, so the baby can more easily pass through the pelvis and birth canal, or vagina. It may take just a few hours, or as long as a few days, to give birth to a baby.

Immediately after birth, the mother's breasts are ready with nutrient-rich milk for her infant. Mother's milk has many other important materials in it, such as antibodies—germ-fighting substances to protect the baby from illness until its own body can do so. In most cases, a mother's breasts will make milk for as long as her baby nurses.

After a baby is born, a woman's reproductive system will eventually go back to its usual monthly cycles. It may take just a month to do so, or several months. Breastfeeding a baby can prevent ovulation for a while, because nerves in the breasts send signals to

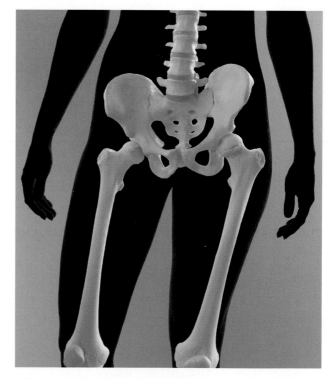

The bones of a woman's hips will move slightly and widen to accommodate the growing fetus in the womb.

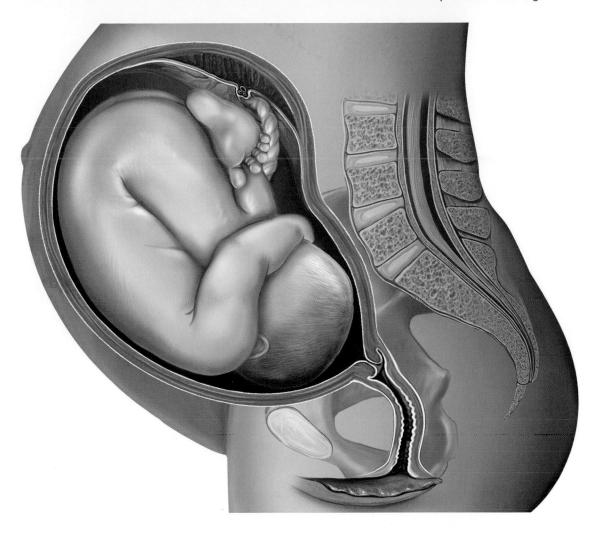

At around thirty-six to thirty-eight weeks, a baby has usually grown as much as it can in the womb, and positions itself for delivery through the birth canal.

the brain that a baby is nursing. Those signals, in turn, keep the pituitary from making the surges of LH and FSH that cause eggs to ovulate. Sometimes, however, ovulation begins to occur sooner than expected, so new mothers should be aware that it may be possible to get pregnant again while nursing.

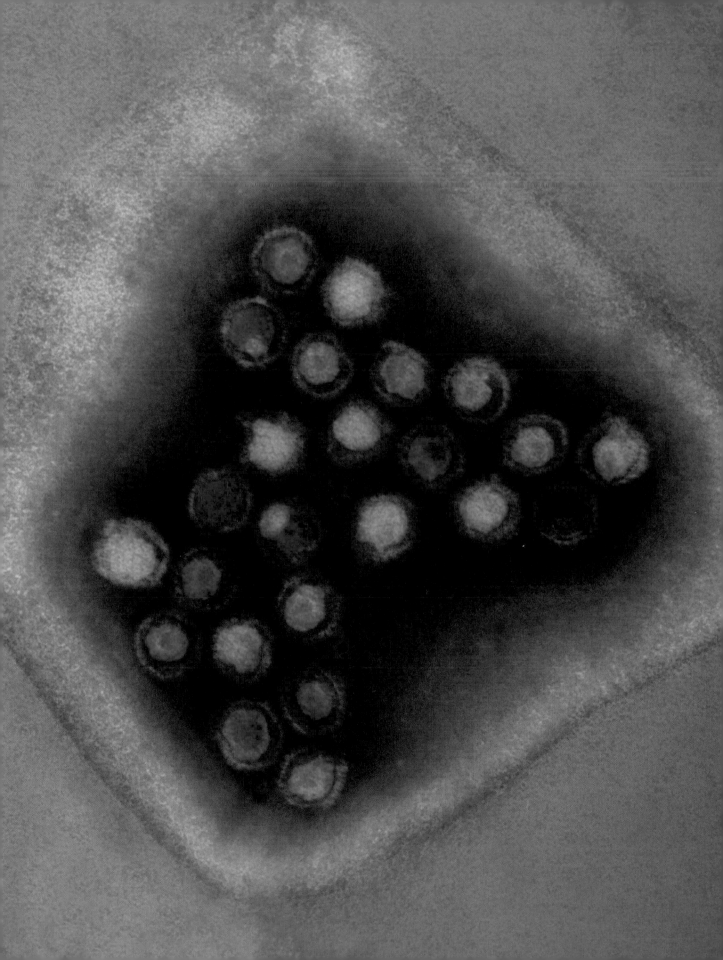

4

Problems with the Reproductive System

The reproductive system, like other parts of the body, can be injured, infected with germs, or develop diseases. Many problems that arise can be cured with medications, surgery, or other medical treatments. However, some of the infections that are spread by sexual contact are incurable and deadly.

INFECTION

It is normal to have certain kinds of harmless bacteria and yeast—which are a type of simple cell—on the skin. Sometimes they become

Herpes simplex is a type of virus that can cause sexually transmitted disease (STD).

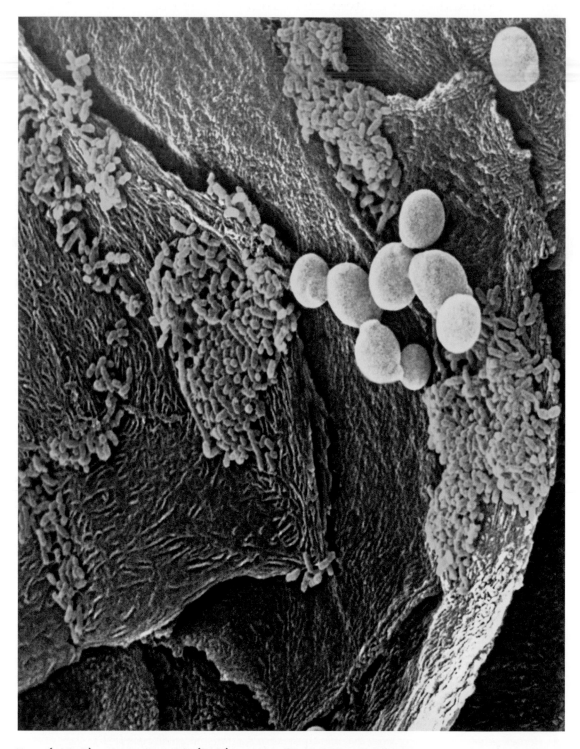

Yeast (yellow) and other bacteria (blue) are normally found in and around the vagina. However, when the yeast and bacteria become too numerous, an infection may develop.

too plentiful and cause an itchy rash around the genitals. They can work their way inside the vagina and urethra, too. Women who are having sexual intercourse get infections more often, because germs on the skin are pushed inside the vagina. Men sometimes get a skin rash around the scrotum and legs especially due to yeast or microscopic fungus that thrive on moist, warm skin. These kinds of infections often clear up on their own in a few days. But sometimes they require medication. A person who notices these symptoms should see a doctor to make sure that it is a simple yeast infection.

SEXUALLY TRANSMITTED DISEASES

Many kinds of illnesses are caused by germs—bacteria and viruses—that can be spread from one person to another. The common cold is a good example of an illness caused by a virus that is passed from a sick person to others by coughing, sneezing, and sharing beverages. Other more serious kinds of diseases are passed by sexual contact. These are known as sexually transmitted diseases (STDs) or venereal diseases (VDs). Many of them injure just the reproductive organs, and can be cured by antibiotics, which are medications that kill or slow the spread of bacteria. Those STDs caused by viruses, however, are hard or impossible to get rid of. While some STDs are short-lived, some can be very harmful and even deadly. The best way to avoid STDs is to not have sexual intercourse or engage in any kind of sexual activity with someone who is or might be infected. People who are sexually active, should be regularly tested for STDs so that they can be treated and can prevent spreading diseases to other.

Chlamydia

In the United States, *Chlamydia trachomatis* is the most common STD-causing bacteria, infecting more than a million people a year. Chlamydia

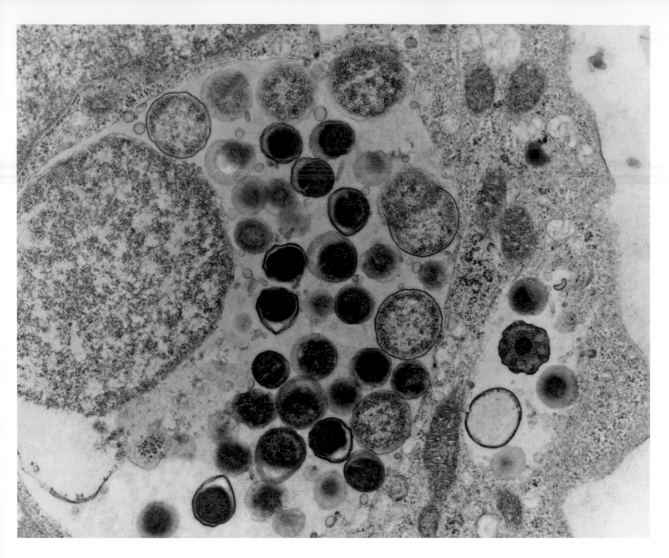

A magnified image shows Chlamydia bacteria (blue) infecting a once-healthy cell.

infection has symptoms of tenderness or pain of the urethra, vagina, testes, rectum, or pelvic area, and sometimes causes fever and nausea. But some people never feel these things, and only learn they are infected during a check-up with a doctor. In women, Chlamydia can lead to pelvic inflammatory disease (PID), which is a serious infection that can damage the uterus and oviducts so badly that the woman cannot get pregnant. Babies whose mothers have Chlamydia may get serious eye or lung infections soon after birth, because they were infected during the birth process. Fortunately, it is easy to test both men and women for Chlamydia, and to cure it with antibiotics.

Gonorrhea

The bacteria *Neisseria gonorrhoeae* cause an STD called gonorrhea. In men, the bacteria irritate the urethra and make it painful to urinate. The same happens in women, who also may have pain or bleeding in the uterus and vagina. The infection can sometimes damage organs enough to cause sterility, which is the inability to make sperm or eggs. Gonorrhea used to be quite common, but the invention of antibiotics in the 1950s changed that. Unfortunately, though, some of the bacteria are becoming resistant to antibiotics, and they survive even after a person is treated. In addition, people who do not know they have the illness, or who cannot get antibiotics that work, continue to spread it to others.

Syphilis

Another kind of bacteria, *Treponema pallidum*, causes syphilis. Syphilis starts out as a painless, red sore on the genitals or anal area, or, in women, inside the vagina. The sore heals after several weeks, but the bacteria may still linger and spread internally for many years, causing damage to the brain, eyes, heart, bones, and other non-reproductive structures. The damage may not be noticed before it is very serious. So someone who thought the bacteria were gone may, years later, become paralyzed, blind, mentally impaired, or may even die. Syphilis is dangerous to fetuses, too. In 2006 about 350 fetuses died of syphilis because they were infected while in the womb. Antibiotics can kill the bacteria, so with a doctor's care, the infection can usually be stopped.

Genital Herpes

A group of very common viruses, the herpes viruses, can infect a few different parts of the body, including the reproductive system. The viruses settle into the skin of the genitals or inside the vagina. Some people have only a mild reaction, and may not notice any problem at all. But other people get painful blisters that take a few weeks to heal, and which come back every few months or years. Genital herpes is similar to the "cold sores" or "fever blisters" that some people get on their lips, which are also caused by a herpes virus. If a fetus is infected by the virus, it can become severely and permanently deformed.

Health experts think that as many as half of all adults may carry the genital herpes virus. Many people do not realize they have it, and unknowingly spread it to others. People with herpes should never have sexual contact while they have a sore. Even after a sore has healed, viruses might be passed to a partner during sexual intercourse. No medications can remove the viruses altogether, but some can make the blisters go away sooner.

Genital Warts

The most common disease-causing viruses that are spread through sexual contact are the human papillomaviruses (HPV). Most people who get the virus do not develop health problems, because their immune systems kill off the viruses. In fact, most people are not aware that they harbor the viruses in their bodies. But some people do develop genital warts, which are small bumps on the skin of the genital area. They are usually painless, and may go away on their own. They may also become more plentiful over time. Though half of all men and women are infected with HPV, only about 1 percent have genital warts. Genital warts do not become cancer, although a different type of HPV can cause cancer.

HIV AND AIDS

The most dangerous of all sexually transmitted diseases is AIDS, which stands for acquired immune deficiency syndrome. "Immune deficiency"

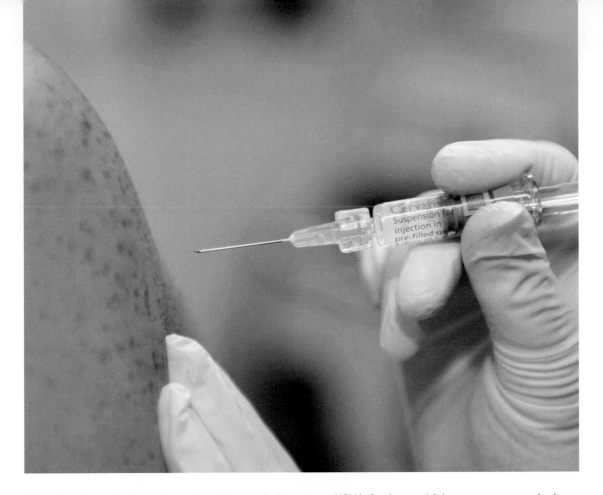

Scientists have developed vaccines that can help prevent HPV infections, which may cause cervical cancer.

means that the immune system is not working well enough to keep a person healthy. The immune system is a team of special cells and chemicals that kill germs, as well as abnormal cells that sometimes appear in healthy organs. In AIDS, the cells of the immune system are destroyed by a virus—called HIV (human immunodeficiency virus)—before they can get rid of it. One way that HIV is passed among people is through sexual contact, because the virus is in the moist fluids of the reproductive organs. (HIV can also be spread through blood—sharing needles used to inject drugs or using untested blood in transfusions and surgery.) Some babies are born with the virus, because they got it from their infected mothers during pregnancy.

A person who is newly infected with HIV will usually have symptoms like those of the flu, including muscle aches, a fever, chills, headache, and

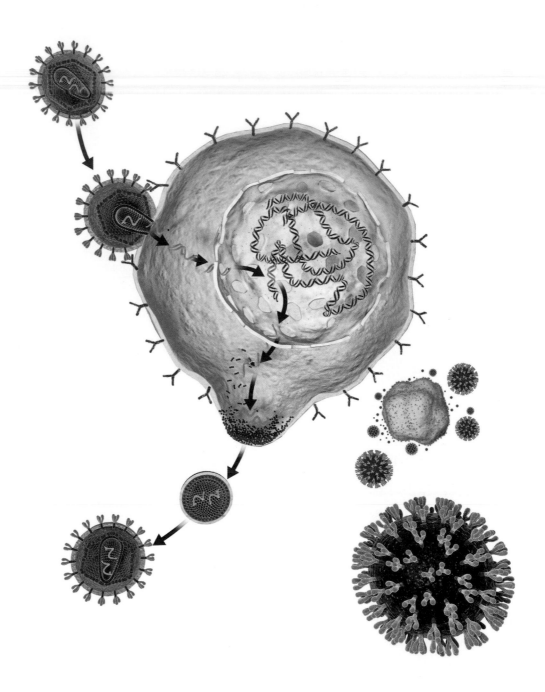

This diagram show how HIV infects a cell, destroys it, and then spreads to other cells.

feeling tired. But those symptoms usually go away in a few weeks. The real danger is that the virus may still be spreading through the body. Over many months and even years, the viruses can work their way into cells and organs of the immune system, gradually killing them. They also can infect the brain, heart, and other vital organs. Then, new symptoms of AIDS start showing up. The most common symptom is getting very sick repeatedly, and with many different illnesses, because the immune system is too weak to fight off germs. Bacterial infections of the lungs, called pneumonia, is the most common cause of death in people with AIDS.

AIDS Today

AIDS is a deadly epidemic that continues to thrive in many parts of the world. Currently, about forty million people worldwide are believed to be infected with HIV, and about four million more become infected each year. Nearly three million people die of AIDS each year. Millions of children and babies, especially in developing countries where medical care is limited, are now orphans because both their parents have died of AIDS.

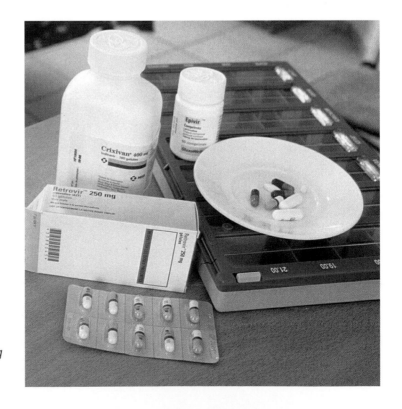

Many people infected with HIV can take medications that may slow down the virus and prolong their lives.

In the United States, about half a million people are infected, and nearly forty thousand new cases are reported each year. About fifteen thousand people die of AIDS in the United States in each year. Advances in medical care can now keep people with HIV alive and in good health longer than ever before--often for many years. But the medications are very expensive, and many people cannot afford them. However, medications do not always save an infected person from dying of AIDS.

The best "treatment" for AIDS is to prevent the spread of the virus in the first place. That means every person should avoid sexual contact unless there is a protective barrier separating reproductive organs and fluids, such as a latex condom covering the penis. A condom is an inexpensive barrier that should always be used whenever semen might come into contact with genitals or anal areas. Even if a person says they do not have the virus, they still may. Not everyone realizes they already have the virus, and some people may lie about having the virus. Prevention and protection is one of the best ways to fight the spread of HIV and AIDS.

CANCER

Cancer is a disease in which a group of abnormal cells begin making many copies of themselves, gradually forming a lump, or tumor. The cells may also spread elsewhere in the body and form tumors there. There are many possible reasons cells might act this way, but also many unsolved mysteries about cancer. Just about any part of the body can develop cancer, including parts of the reproductive system. Sometimes it can be treated, but other times, the disease is fatal.

Cancer is treated in different ways, depending on where it is, how large the tumor is, how the cells are behaving, and also on how the person wants to combat the disease. Usually, the first step is to remove the tumor, or sometimes the whole organ in which it is located, by surgery. Then, many patients take cancer-killing drugs (chemotherapy) or have radiation treatments for some weeks, in an effort to kill any cancer cells the surgery did not remove.

Cancer in Women

The most common place for cancer in the female reproductive system is in a breast or both of them. Many women survive breast cancer, but some do not. Some women have a gene—a part of their cells' genetic material—that makes breast cells behave abnormally and form tumors. But only a small percentage of women who get breast cancer have that gene. For most women, the cause is unknown. Scientists are currently studying how chemicals are involved in causing breast cancer.

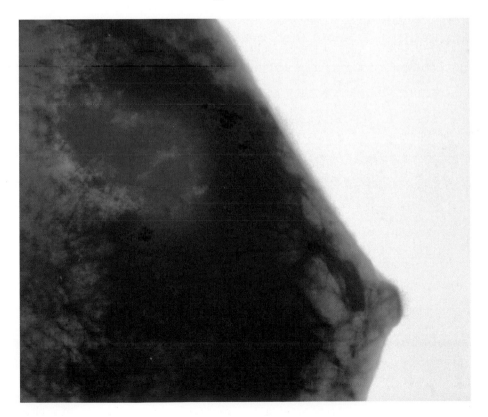

Breast exams and X rays called mammograms can help detect breast cancer (pinkish purple).

Women also get cancer in their ovaries or the uterus, especially the cervix, which is the part of the uterus that connects with the vagina. It is hard to tell if a woman has ovarian cancer, because the ovaries are deep within the pelvis. But the cervix can be checked easily for signs of cervical cancer by a procedure called a PAP test. A doctor or nurse tests a small sample of cells from the cervix to see if they look abnormal. The cause of nearly all cervical cancers is a type of human papillomavirus (HPV). HPV gets into the vagina and uterus of women from infected men. But most women never develop cancer. Abnormal cells can be killed if they are found early enough, but if a tumor has formed, the uterus may need to be removed. In ovarian cancer, ovaries and uterus usually are removed in the hopes of getting rid of every trace of the cancer.

Cancer in Men

The most common kind of cancer of the male reproductive system is prostate cancer. The prostate gland surrounds the urethra, the tube

Tumors on the prostate (right) are definite signs of prostate cancer. Checkups with doctors and special scans may show these tumors before they grow too large.

through which urine leaves the body. A tumor can block the urethra and make it hard for the man to release urine. However, nearly every man's prostate grows a bit as he ages, without it being cancer. Doctors check for signs of prostate cancer regularly. They feel where the prostate is, to see if it is especially large or oddly shaped. They also check a sample of blood for a chemical called PSA, or prostatic specific antigen. PSA is a protein made by cancer cells of the prostate. If there is PSA in the blood sample, it is a warning that cancer is developing. Prostate cancer is treated by surgically removing the prostate gland, and sometimes with chemotherapy and radiation.

INFERTILITY

Some couples have problems having babies. This problem is called infertility. Doctors who specialize in infertility help couples discover what the problem is. It may be that the woman's oviducts are damaged from pelvic inflammatory disease (PID) and eggs cannot pass. Or the man's sperm may be abnormally shaped and move too slowly. Or, reproductive hormones may not be plentiful enough or made at the right time. Doctors have devised many creative ways to help a couple get pregnant. The methods can be very expensive and difficult, and may not always work.

One method of treating infertility is called *in vitro* fertilization A woman may be given medication with hormones in it to make many eggs ovulate at once. When more eggs are present, it is more likely that one will get fertilized. But sometimes as many as five, six, or more eggs get fertilized, and go on to develop as babies. It can be very dangerous for a woman to carry that many babies at once, since it can be a serious health risk to her and the babies—each baby will only be a fraction of what a normal-size baby would be.

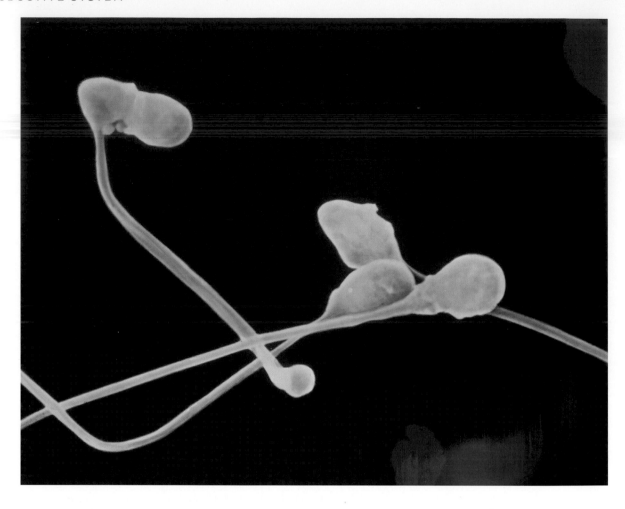

Deformed and misshapen sperm usually cannot successfully fertilize an egg. Fertility problems in men are sometimes caused by abnormal sperm.

A way to avoid this problem is to collect the many ovulated eggs and fertilize them with the man's sperm in vitro. *In vitro* means "in glass" in Latin, and the procedure is called in vitro fertilization because sperm and eggs meet in a glass dish. Those that become fertilized are allowed to develop for a few days, and then a few are placed in the woman's uterus. Often, but not always, this works to make one or two healthy babies. A different problem, though, is that any fertilized eggs that were not used must be kept frozen indefinitely, because it is illegal to dispose of them. Many difficult legal battles are brewing over who "owns" them, and what to do with them.

If there is a problem with a woman's uterus, or she cannot carry a baby for nine months, a surrogate may be used. A surrogate is a woman who is implanted with a fertilized egg, and ends up giving birth to the baby.

Some couples that want a baby may decide to adopt a child who needs a home. There are many stories of such couples that, once they are a family, get the surprising news a few years later that the woman has become pregnant after all. No one really knows why that happens, but one idea is that the man and woman can finally relax and enjoy being parents, and that perhaps the brain, which is where emotions happen and reproductive hormones are controlled, somehow manages to restore fertility.

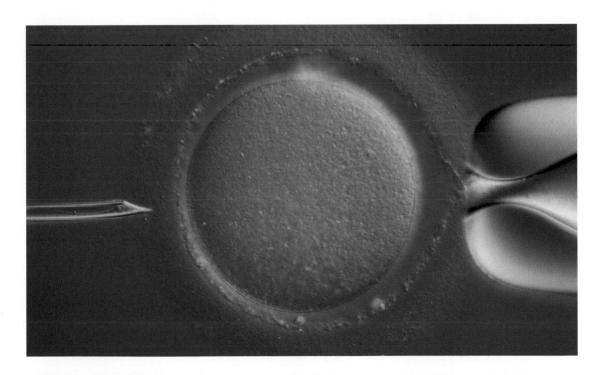

Special reproductive technologies allow doctors to fertilize an egg outside of the body and then implant it into a healthy womb.

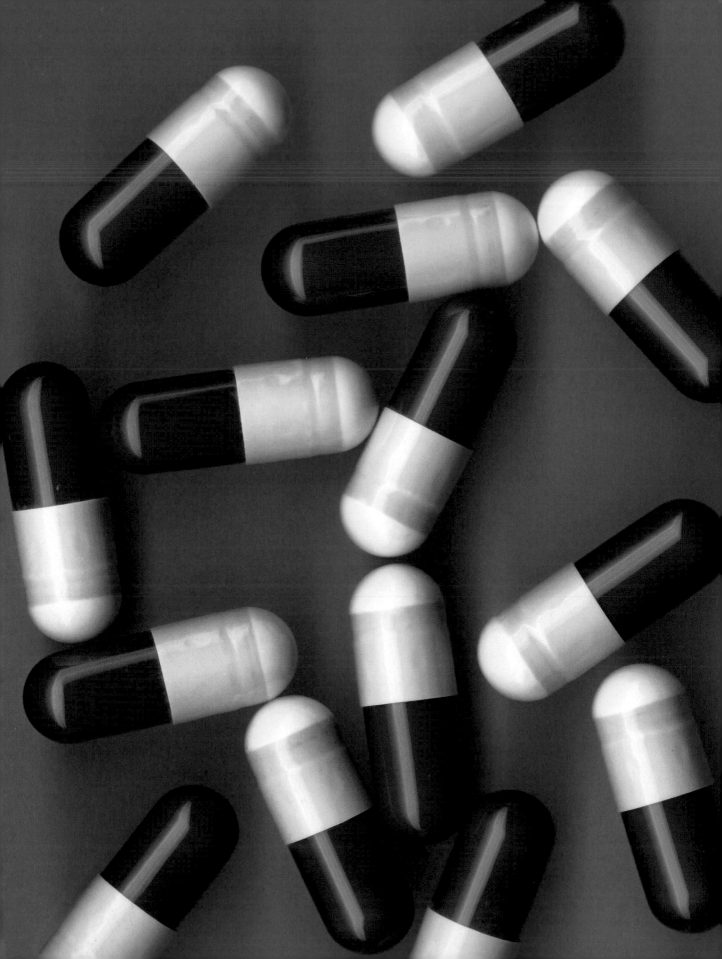

5

Caring for the Reproductive System

T he reproductive system can be affected many problems. Because most problems of the reproductive system are diseases spread by sexual contact, the surest way to avoid them is abstinence, which is not having sexual contact with anybody. Many people decide to wait to have sex until they find someone they care about deeply and trust. Even then, one must take steps to practice "safe sex," which prevents spreading sexually transmitted diseases and starting unwanted pregnancies.

SAFE SEX

Many problems with the reproductive system can be treated by medication. It is important to talk to your doctor if you think you are having problems.

Aside from abstinence, condoms are the best form of protection against both STDs and pregnancy. A condom is made of stretchy, thin material that covers a man's penis completely and has a place at the tip where semen can collect. It forms a barrier which, when used properly, keeps semen away from anything else.

When used correctly, condoms prevent pregnancy 98 percent of the time. There are many different types and brands of condoms that block pregnancy. Only those made of latex or polyurethane are proven to be a good barrier to bacteria and viruses, including HIV.

BIRTH CONTROL

Every year, thousands of women discover they are pregnant when they did not wish to be. The number of abortions done each year gives some idea how often this happens. An abortion ends pregnancy by removing the fetus from the woman's uterus. More than 800,000 legal abortions are done each year in the United States, and some are done illegally as well. Many experts believe that most unwanted pregnancies could have been prevented with birth control. Birth control really means "fertilization control," which is keeping eggs and sperm apart. Birth control is also called contraception.

The most reliable birth control method is abstinence—avoiding sexual intercourse. It is still possible that if the man ejaculates outside a woman's body near her genitals, sperm may make their way into her vagina and fertilize an egg, but that is very rare.

Some birth control methods use barriers to block sperm and egg from meeting. A condom that fits on the man's penis is the most common and effective. A "female condom" is a latex sheet that covers the vagina. Both types of condoms also protect against STDs. Another barrier is a diaphragm or cervical cap, which is a flexible latex cup that holds a spermicide (sperm-killing chemical) and fits over the woman's cervix to

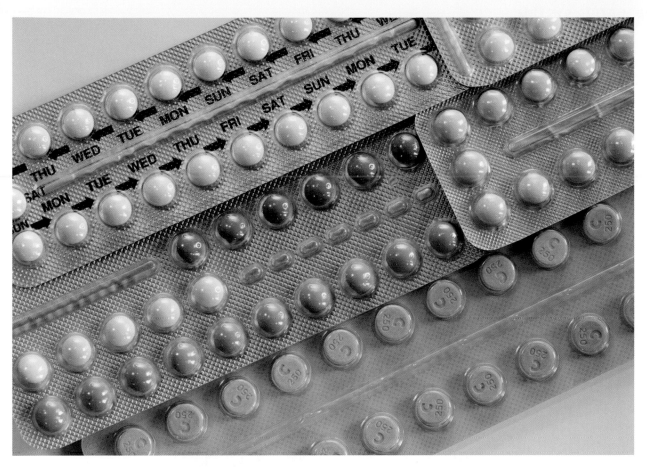

One form of birth control is a set of pills that must be taken every day to regulate a woman's hormones.

block sperm from getting into the uterus. Diaphragms are cervical caps that are put in and removed by the woman each time she has intercourse. They do nothing to protect against STDs.

Another common birth control method is medication that a woman takes to disrupt her menstrual cycle. Such medications come in many forms—pills, patches worn on the skin, injections, or items placed in the vagina or uterus. They contain sex steroids that interrupt a woman's normal hormone levels, which stops her ovaries from making mature eggs, and usually stops her from having menstrual bleeding. Some women may use birth control to regulate their menstrual cycles or treat problems associated with menstruation. However, taking these medications may have serious health risks for some, such as a higher chance of having heart attack or life-threatening blockage of a blood vessel, and cancer of the female reproductive organs. They do nothing to protect against STDs.

Sometimes a man or woman who is certain he or she does not want any or any more children chooses surgical sterilization. That means having the reproductive ducts closed so that sperm or eggs cannot travel anywhere. A doctor can tie off or cut a man's ductus deferentia in a simple surgery called a vasectomy. A woman can have her oviducts cut or tied off in a more complicated surgery. This is called tubal ligation.

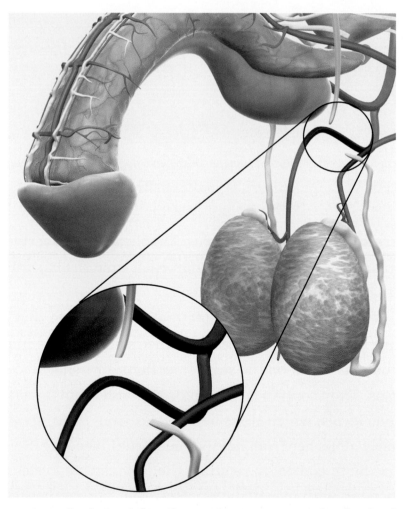

During a vasectomy, the ductus deferentia are cut to prevent sperm from leaving the body.

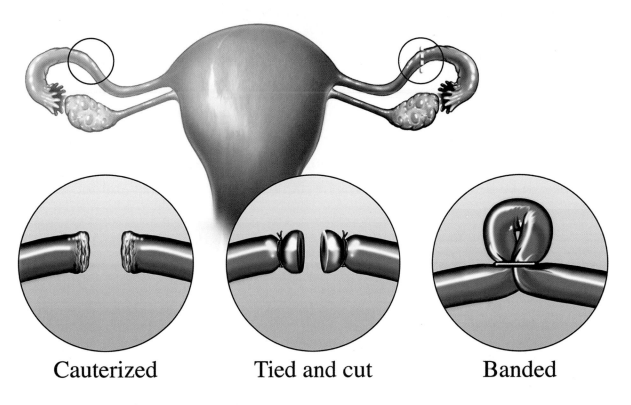

Cauterized   Tied and cut   Banded

Tubal ligation may be carried out by cauterizing (sealing) the fallopian tubes, cutting and tying them, or folding and banding them.

The least successful type of birth control is when a couple simply tries to control when ejaculation will happen while having intercourse. The plan is for the man to pull his penis away from the woman's vagina just before he ejaculates, or to use his "will power" to prevent ejaculation from happening at all. These are very difficult things to do. The sexual sensations that a man feels are very powerful and can trigger ejaculation suddenly. In addition, small amounts of sperm-containing fluid are made by the penis long before ejaculation. Another problem is that many couples, in the middle of intercourse, prefer not to stop. They decide to take a risk, allowing the man to ejaculate, only to find some weeks later that the woman is pregnant.

ENDING A PREGNANCY

In the United States, women who become pregnant have the legal right to end the pregnancy by abortion. It is important for a woman considering abortion to talk right away with a nurse or doctor, and also with someone who can help make the difficult decision about whether abortion is the right step. Some people end, or terminate, a pregnancy when the fetus is very ill or if the pregnancy will be dangerous for the fetus and for the mother.

There are several methods of abortion. Medical abortion means taking medications that disturb the woman's reproductive hormones and make the uterus contract, so the fetus and endometrium are shed from the uterus. The medications work only during about the first nine weeks when the fetus and placenta are small. They can cause nausea, vomiting, severe cramps, dizziness, and heavy bleeding from the uterus. Other medications, called the "morning after" pill or "plan B," prevent a fertilized egg from implanting in the uterus in the first place. They must be taken within a few days after having unprotected sex. Such medications are not a good substitute for birth control, and they do nothing to halt the spread of STDs. Other abortion methods may be necessary after the first few weeks of pregnancy. They are done by a doctor or specially trained nurse, who uses tools to vacuum or scrape the inside of the uterus, removing the fetus, placenta, and endometrium.

GOOD HYGIENE

Cleansing the genitals helps keep germs from working their way into the reproductive system. No special chemicals are needed. Simply washing with soap and warm water, and then drying the skin thoroughly, works well. For females, it is best to keep soap out of the vagina. Although special liquids are sold for cleansing inside the vagina, such liquids actu-

It is important to keep the groin area—and external reproductive organs—clean. To prevent irritation, plain soap without fragrances or dyes should be used.

ally lower the vagina's natural germ-killing moisture. Even with good cleaning, many people sometimes notice itching, stinging, an odor, or pain while using the toilet. In those cases, a doctor should look at the area, since there may be an infection that medications could easily clear up.

TALKING BEFORE DOING

It is especially important that people talk about how they are going to prevent pregnancy and spreading STDs *before* they start to explore each other sexually. And even though a partner claims to be disease-free, many people harbor bacteria or viruses without knowing it. To truly remain safe, the only reason to have "unprotected sex" (using no condom or birth control) is to intentionally create a baby. Even then, partners should first have a doctor check them for any infections that could be cleared up with medications.

Young people and even sexually experienced adults may not believe they can really make a baby in just a few minutes of sexual contact. Teenagers or preteens in puberty may not even realize their bodies are already making sperm and eggs. Fortunately, today's young people, more than any generation before them, are learning the facts about reproduction and how to prevent pregnancy and STDs. It is up to them to put that knowledge to practice.

Glossary

AIDS (Acquired Immune Deficiency Syndrome)—A deadly illness caused by a human immunodeficiency virus (HIV), which is spread among people whose semen, vaginal moisture, genitals or anal areas come into contact.

blastocyst—A ball of cells that forms from a fertilized egg, and which settles into the uterus and begins developing into a fetus.

contraception—Birth control.

ductus deferens (vas deferens)—A tube that carries sperm from the testes to the urethra.

ejaculation—A powerful release of semen from the penis.

endometrium—The layer of the uterus that is shed during menstrual flow, and provides nutrients and blood to a fetus during pregnancy.

fertilization—The moment that a sperm combines with an egg.

fetus—A baby that is still in the mother's uterus.

follicle-stimulating hormone (FSH)—One of the pituitary's hormones that controls reproduction.

gametes—Eggs or sperm.

genitals—The parts of the reproductive system that are visible between the legs.

HIV—Human immunodeficiency virus, which causes AIDS.

human chorionic gonadotropin (hCG)—A hormone made by the placenta that keeps a pregnant woman's body able to nourish the fetus.

hypothalamus—A region of the brain that controls the pituitary gland.

in vitro fertilization—A medical procedure in which eggs and sperm are mixed in a dish, and fertilized eggs put into a woman's uterus.

labia—Folds of skin that are part of female genitalia.

luteinizing hormone (LH)—One of the pituitary's hormones that control reproduction.

menstrual cycle—The monthly changes in hormone levels and activities of the female reproductive system.

myometrium—The muscle layer of the uterus.

oxytocin—A pituitary hormone that causes muscles in the uterus to contract and breasts to release milk.

pituitary—A hormone-releasing gland in the brain that controls much of reproduction.

placenta—An organ that forms between the uterus and a developing baby and provides all its nutritional needs..

prolactin—A pituitary hormone that causes a pregnant woman's breasts to make milk.

prostate— A pair of organs that help make semen.

seminal vesicles—An organ that forms between the uterus and a developing baby and provides all its nutritional needs..

seminiferous tubules—Microscopic tubes inside the testes where sperm develop.

Sertoli cells—Large cells among developing sperm that provide them with nutrients.

sex steroids—Reproductive hormones (testosterone, estrogen, progesterone) that cause male or female features.

STD (Sexually transmitted disease)—Any disease spread among people whose genitals, semen, or vaginal moisture come into contact.

urethra—The tube that empties urine from the body.

uterus—The female reproductive organ where a baby develops (womb).

vagina—The female reproductive organ into which the penis fits during sexual intercourse.

Find Out More

Books

Bledsoe, Karen. *Human Reproduction, Growth, and Development*. Logan, IA: Perfection Learning, 2007.

Lange, Donna. *Taking Responsibility: A Teen's Guide to Contraception and Pregnancy*. Philadelphia, PA: Mason Crest Publishers, 2005.

Miller, Michaela. *Reproduction and Growth*. Detroit, MI: KidHaven Press, 2005.

Silverstein, Alvin and Virginia. *The STDs Update*. Berkeley Heights, NJ: Enslow Elementary, 2006.

Sommers, Michael. *Yeast Infections, Trichomoniasis, and Toxic Shock Syndrome*. New York: Rosen Central, 2008.

Waters, Sophie. *The Female Reproductive System*. New York: Rosen Publishing Group, 2007.

Websites

AIDS: Staying Alive
http://www.staying-alive.org/en/home

Birth Control and Contraception for Teenagers
http://www.avert.org/cpills.htm

Female Reproductive System
http://kidshealth.org/parent/general/body_basics/female_reproductive_
   system.html

Life in the Fast Lane
http://www.teenageparent.org

Male Reproductive System
http://kidshealth.org/parent/general/body_basics/male_reproductive.html

NOVA Online: Life's Greatest Miracle
http://www.pbs.org/wgbh/nova/miracle

Teens' Health: Sexual Health
http://www.kidshealth.org/teen/sexual_health

Index

implantation, 41–43

in vitro fertilization, 62–63, **62**

infection, 49–51

infertility, 61–63

labia, **24**, 26

LH, 22, 36, 37, **37**, 46

menstrual cycle, 25, 36–37, 46

ovaries, 10, 11, 13, **13**, 15, 16, **16**, **17**, 19, **20**, 21, 35

oviducts, 19,

ovulation, 19

ovum *see* egg

pelvic inflammatory disease (PID), 52

pelvis *see* hips

penis, 29–30, **30**, 32–33

pituitary, 22–23, **23**, 37

placenta, 43–44, **43**

pregnancy, 16, 19, 44–45, **45**, 69–71

prostaglandin, 32

prostate

cancer, 60, **60**

gland, 32

puberty, 8, 10–11, **11**, 13, 37

scrotum, 27, 32

semen, 32

seminal vesicles, 32

seminiferous tubules, 27, 28, **28**, 31

Sertoli cells, 29, 29

sex steroids, 11–12

see also estrogen, progesterone, testosterone

sexually transmitted disease (STD), **48**, 49–58, **50**, **52**, **55**, **57**, **58**

sperm, **4**, 8, 9, **14**, 19, 27, 28, 28, 29, 29, 31, 32, 33, 37–40, 39, 37–38, 39–40, 39

sterilization, 67–69, 68, 69

syphilis, 53–54

testes, 10, 12, **12**, 22, 26–27, **27**, 32, 38

testosterone, 8, 12, 29

tubal ligation, 68–69, **69**

urethra, 31, 51

About the Author

Lorrie Klosterman is a science writer and educator who earned a Bachelor of Science degree from Oregon State University and a Doctoral Degree from the University of California at Berkeley, both in the field of zoology (the study of animal life, including humans). She has taught courses in human health and disease to college and nursing students for several years, and writes about health for a magazine in New York's Hudson Valley. Lorrie Klosterman has also written several health-related books for young adults. Her greatest joy comes from experiencing and learning about the amazing world of animals and plants, and sharing those experiences with others.